Presented to

Batavia Public Library District By

Pearl Blass

In Memory of

ELEANOR JONES

8/98

MOM AND ME

PICTURES AND WORDS BY

MIELA FORD

GREENWILLOW BOOKS NEW YORK

The full-color photographs were reproduced from 35-mm slides.
The text type is ITC Kabel Medium.
Copyright © 1998 by Miela Ford
All rights reserved. No part of this book may be reproduced
or utilized in any form or by any means, electronic
or mechanical, including photocopying, recording,
or by any information storage and retrieval system,
without permission in writing from the Publisher, Greenwillow Books,
a division of William Morrow & Company, Inc.,
1350 Avenue of the Americas, New York, NY 10019.
www.williammorrow.com
Printed in Singapore by Tien Wah Press
First Edition
10 9 8 7 6 5 4 3 2 1

LIBRARY OF CONGRESS CATALOGING-IN-PUBLICATION DATA
Ford, Miela
Mom and me / by Miela Ford.
p.   cm.
Summary: A mother polar bear and her child sleep, play, and eat together.
ISBN 0-688-15889-7 (trade).   ISBN 0-688-15890-0 (lib. bdg.)
[1. Polar bears—Fiction.   2. Bears—Fiction.   3. Mother and child—Fiction.]
I. Title.   PZ7.F75322Mo   1998   [E]—dc21   97-31411   CIP   AC

FOR MAX

I'm awake.

My mom's asleep.

Should I wake her up?

Come on, Mom!

Get up with me.

Let's go.

I want to play.

Roly-poly,

poly-roly.

In . . .

and out.

Heads . . .

and tails. Ka-boom!

I can follow.

Can I lead?

A push.

I'm off.

A call.

I'm back.

And just in time for lunch.